EXPLORING WORLD CULTURES

Cuba

Laura L. Sullivan

Cavendish
Square

New York

Published in 2020 by Cavendish Square Publishing, LLC
243 5th Avenue, Suite 136, New York, NY 10016

Website: cavendishsq.com

This publication represents the opinions and views of the author based on his or her personal experience, knowledge, and research. The information in this book serves as a general guide only. The author and publisher have used their best efforts in preparing this book and disclaim liability rising directly or indirectly from the use and application of this book.

All websites were available and accurate when this book was sent to press.

Library of Congress Cataloging-in-Publication Data

Names: Sullivan, Laura L., 1974- author.
Title: Cuba / Laura L. Sullivan.
Description: First edition. | New York : Cavendish Square, [2020] |
Series: Exploring world cultures | Includes bibliographical references and index.
Identifiers: LCCN 2019010036 (print) | LCCN 2019010686 (ebook) |
ISBN 9781502651754 (ebook) | ISBN 9781502651747 (library bound) | ISBN 9781502651723 (pbk.) |
ISBN 9781502651730 (6 pack)
Subjects: LCSH: Cuba--Juvenile literature.
Classification: LCC F1758.5 (ebook) | LCC F1758.5 .S83 2020 (print) | DDC 972.91--dc23
LC record available at https://lccn.loc.gov/2019010036

Editor: Lauren Miller
Copy Editor: Nathan Heidelberger
Associate Art Director: Alan Sliwinski
Designer: Christina Shults
Production Coordinator: Karol Szymczuk
Photo Research: J8 Media

The photographs in this book are used by permission and through the courtesy of:

Cover, Akturer/Shutterstock.com; p. 5 Kriangkrai Thitimakorn/Moment/Getty Images; p. 6 Peter Hermes Furian/iStock/
Getty Images; p. 7 Salvador Aznar/Shutterstock.com; p. 8 © North Wind Picture Archives; p. 9 Universal History Archive/
UIG/Getty Images; p. 10 ERNESTO MASTRASCUSA/POOL/AFP/Getty Images; p. 11 YAMIL LAGE/AFP/Getty Images; p. 12
Taylor S. Kennedy/National Geographic Image Collection/Getty Images; p. 13 Hugh Sitton/Corbis/Getty Images; p. 14 Jeff
Mondragon/Alamy Stock Photo; p. 15 Ger Bosma/Moment Open/Getty Images; p. 16 Denys Turavtsov/Shutterstock.com;
p. 17 Prisma by Dukas/UIG/Getty Images; p. 18 Anna Isakova/ITAR-TASS News Agency/Alamy; p. 19 Atlantide Phototravel/
Corbis/Getty Images; p. 20 Felix Lipov/Alamy Stock Photo; p.21 Roberto Machado Noa/LightRocket/Getty Images; p. 22
Michele Burgess/Alamy Stock Photo; p. 24 Christopher Pillitz/The Image Bank/Getty Images; p. 26 Charles NorPeet/Getty
Images; p. 28 Antony Souter/Alamy Stock Photo; p. 29 Bonchan/iStock/Getty Images.

Printed in the United States of America

Contents

Introduction

Cuba is an island nation. It is located in a part of the world called the Caribbean. The people of Cuba are of Native American, European, and African descent.

Cuba has a **socialist** style of government and economy. It is designed to help the people. However, it is not perfect. There are food shortages. Sometimes, Cuban citizens are not treated fairly. Many Cubans have moved to the United States to have a better life.

Still, Cuba is a vibrant country. The people are friendly and hardworking. In cities like Havana, there is music and dancing every night. There are also delicious foods to eat.

Tourists from around the world visit this country to enjoy Cuba's beautiful beaches. They can also learn a lot when they travel to Cuba and talk to the people who live there. It is not always easy to travel to Cuba, so it can be helpful and fun to read about this country too.

Let's explore Cuba!

Downtown Havana is colorful and vibrant.

Cuba is located right where the Atlantic Ocean, the Gulf of Mexico, and the Caribbean Sea meet. It is about 93 miles (150 kilometers) away from Florida.

This map shows Cuba and its many neighbors.

Cuba is the biggest island in the Caribbean. It has around 2,320 miles (3,735 km) of coastline. Havana is the capital city of Cuba. It is also the biggest city on the island.

FACT!

Cuba has a lot of hurricanes between August and October.

Most of Cuba is low and flat, with small hills. There are some mountains. They are found in the southeast. Pico Turquino is the highest point on the island, at 6,476 feet

Hurricanes bring strong winds and sometimes heavy rain.

(1,974 meters). The Cauto is the longest of three major rivers in Cuba.

Cuba has a warm, tropical climate. In the summer, it gets lots of rain and tropical storms.

Island-Hopping

Cuba has more than four thousand islands. Most are very small. They are clustered together in groups called archipelagos.

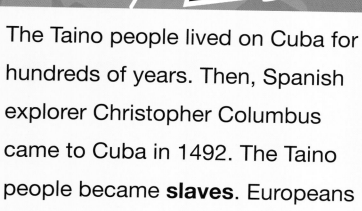

The Taino people lived on Cuba for hundreds of years. Then, Spanish explorer Christopher Columbus came to Cuba in 1492. The Taino people became **slaves**. Europeans gave the Taino sicknesses. Many Taino died.

The Taino lived on Cuba before Europeans came.

Cuba was ruled by Spain until 1898. It then became an independent country, but the United States had a lot of power over what happened on the island.

Several Taino words are used in English, including iguana, canoe, hurricane, and hammock.

José Martí

José Martí (1853–1895) is a Cuban national hero. He helped lead Cuba's fight for independence. He also wrote poems and essays about freedom.

In 1959, Fidel Castro took control. He made Cuba a communist country. In communism, the government owns all property. People work as much as they can. In return, they are given everything they need to live.

Castro led Cuba for forty-nine years. In 2018, a new constitution was written for Cuba. It limits a president's time in office to two terms that can each last for five years.

Fidel Castro during a visit to the United States in 1959

Cuba's official name is the Republic of Cuba. The Communist Party of Cuba controls the government. The government has three parts, or branches: executive, legislative, and judicial.

In 2019, Raúl Castro (Fidel's brother) was the leader of Cuba.

The first secretary of the Communist Party has the most power. Below them is the president. These positions make up the executive branch.

FACT!

In Cuba, all people sixteen and older can vote, so long as they have not been convicted of a crime.

Sharing Power

Cuba's new constitution added the position of prime minister. This spreads power more evenly within the executive branch.

The legislative branch includes the Council of State and the National Assembly of People's Power. They make the laws. The judicial branch is made up of courts. The

Cubans over the age of sixteen can vote.

highest court is the People's Supreme Court.

Today, Cuba is more of a socialist country. This means that the people can own things like property, factories, and farms. However, Cuba's government is still strict. It controls and limits people's freedom.

The Cuban government controls the economy. This is because the government owns most of the factories and farms in Cuba. Recently, there has been an increase in

Cuban pesos have pictures of famous Cubans from history.

private ownership. About 22 percent of Cubans work for private companies and farms.

FACT!

The United States currently has an **embargo** against Cuba. This means the US does not buy from or trade with the island.

Cuban money is called the peso. There are two kinds of peso. One is the Cuban peso. It is used to pay people and to buy most things. The other is the convertible peso. This is used mostly by tourists.

A woman poses for a photo with two flower sellers in Havana.

Cuba sells goods like sugar, fruit, coffee, tobacco, and fish to other countries. Tourism is growing in Cuba. About 4.8 million people visited the island in 2018.

Rations

Many Cubans do not make a lot of money. They use a **ration** book, or *libreta,* to get basic foods like sugar, rice, or cooking oil.

The Environment

Cuba has many different plants and animals. Lots of palm trees and orchids are on the island. The cork palm trees that grow in Cuba are some of the rarest trees in the world.

A West Indian manatee swims in the waters near Cuba.

Birds like flamingos and nightingales live near the rivers. Tortoises and many kinds of frogs live there too. Manatees live along the coast. Rare Cuban crocodiles live in the

FACT!

The blue, white, and red trogon is Cuba's national bird.

The Cuban Hutia

The Cuban hutia is Cuba's biggest land animal. This rodent can reach almost 20 pounds (9 kilograms)!

A Cuban hutia enjoys some fruit.

Zapata Swamp. Cuban rock iguanas climb trees in the forests.

Unfortunately, many forests have been cut down for farming or firewood. Air pollution is another problem. This is because cars in Cuba are very old. The smoke they create is unhealthy. Since the 1980s, the government has been more active in protecting the forests and the environment in general.

Cuban people come from many places, including Europe and Africa. People from different backgrounds often marry each other. Today, it is hard to say how many people of each group live on the island.

Cubans today have ancestors from Europe, Africa, and the Caribbean.

In 2016, about 11.5 million people lived in Cuba. More than two million lived in Havana.

FACT!

The average Cuban person lives to be seventy-nine years old.

Chinese Ancestry

In the nineteenth century, many Chinese citizens came to Cuba to work. Today, more than one hundred thousand Cubans have Chinese ancestry.

This gate marks the entrance to Barrio Chino, or Chinatown, in Havana.

Many Cubans live in the United States. After the communist revolution in 1959, a lot of people went to the United States. People in Cuba could not see their family members who moved there. Today, it is still hard to travel between these two countries.

Cuban law says women are equal with men in politics and at work. It also says they have to be treated equally at home. However, most women are still expected to cook, clean, and take care of children. Because of this, many Cuban women decide to not have children.

Ana María Mari Machado (*front row, second from right*) is an important female politican.

Children must attend school from ages six to sixteen. Students then have to pass tests to

FACT!

In Cuba, 99.75 percent of people know how to read and write.

get into college. Young men also need to spend two years in the **military**. Education in Cuba is free. It is paid for by the government.

Cubans are friendly. They enjoy playing games together.

Family and friends are important in Cuba. Both men and women greet each other with hugs and a kiss on the cheek. Even strangers are greeted as friends.

Religion

Religion is important to many Cubans. Most religious Cubans are Christian. Smaller groups practice other religions. These include Hinduism, Buddhism, Islam, and Judaism.

Sacred Heart of Jesus is one of the oldest churches in Cuba.

Santería is another common religion in Cuba. Its name means "worship of **saints**." Africans brought Santería

Christmas used to be a national holiday in Cuba. However, the communist government did not support religion. In 1969, the government got rid of the holiday.

Regardless of their beliefs, about 80 percent of Cubans go to Santería leaders to get advice about the future, for luck, or for healing.

Our Lady of El Cobre (Charity) is the patron saint of Cuba.

to Cuba. Some people attend both Christian—especially Roman Catholic—and Santería services.

Cubans did not have much religious freedom after the communist revolution. Religious people could not join the Communist Party. After 1992, the constitution was changed to protect people with religious beliefs. More people practice a religion today.

Spanish is Cuba's official language. It is sometimes called Cuban Spanish, or Cubano. Some words are said differently in Cuba than they would be in other countries that use Spanish.

Signs are written in Spanish and sometimes English.

FACT!

Instead of *señor* or *señora* (meaning "sir" or "madam"), many Cubans say *compañero* or *compañera* (meaning "comrade" or "friend").

Friendly Names

It is common to use friendly or loving titles in Cuba. For example, in a store, the cashier might call a customer *mi vida* (my life) or *mi corazón* (my heart).

Cuban Spanish borrows words from other languages. Some words come from the native Taino people. English words are used too. They are slightly different though. For example, Cubans say *chor* for "shorts."

Greetings can be either polite or more relaxed. People use relaxed language with family members and close friends. Polite language is used with older people or strangers. Usually, it is okay to use relaxed words with everyone.

23

Art is a way for people to share their opinions. Some Cuban artists and musicians celebrate Cuba. Others paint, draw, or sing because they want the government to change.

Cuba's many carnivals feature dancing and colorful costumes.

Cuban music blends Spanish and African styles. Popular forms of

FACT!

The Cuban National Ballet School is the largest in the world. Approximately three thousand dancers study there.

music are *son cubano*, habanera, mambo, bolero, rumba, and cha-cha. Many of these styles have their own dance steps too.

Cuba has many festivals during the year. There are jazz festivals, film festivals, and book fairs. On May 1, Cubans celebrate their country, its workers, and socialism. A similar holiday is the Santiago de Cuba Carnival. It is the biggest carnival in Cuba. It is held from July 18 to July 27 and celebrates the communist revolution.

Colorful Streets

Street art is very common in Cuba. There are many paintings on city walls.

Fun and Play

In Cuba, sports are important. Kids are required to learn baseball, volleyball, basketball, gymnastics, and track and field in school. Many Cubans continue to play sports as adults.

Julio Martinez bats for the Cuban national baseball team in a 2016 game.

Baseball is Cuba's national sport. More than half of all Cubans play baseball. When kids get together, it is often to play baseball. Basketball is popular too.

FACT!

Snorkeling and scuba diving are very popular thanks to Cuba's coral reefs.

Special Training

Kids who are good at sports go to special schools on an island called the Isle of Youth. There, they go to school, practice their sport, and work three hours every day in the island's orange groves.

The Cuban national basketball team is the only Caribbean basketball team to win a medal at the Olympics as of 2019.

Boxing and volleyball are also popular in Cuba. Along the coast, Cubans enjoy water sports like swimming, sailing, and paddleboarding.

Cuban food is tasty! Many meals have Spanish, African, or Caribbean ingredients. Meals usually include meat with rice and beans. One example is *arroz con pollo*, or "rice with chicken." *Ropa vieja* ("old clothes") is stewed, shredded beef. Since Cuba is an island, lots of people also eat seafood.

Ropa vieja is Cuba's national dish.

The Cuban sandwich has become very popular in the United States. It is a sandwich with

FACT!

Pasteles are pastries with savory or sweet fillings.

Café Cubano is a popular, small, and very strong coffee drink.

buttered bread, roasted pork, ham, and Swiss cheese. Mustard and a pickle are usually added. Then, the sandwich is pressed and toasted.

Cuban sandwiches are now enjoyed all around the world.

Flan is a dessert of custard with caramel sauce. *Tres leches* ("three milks") cake is a sponge cake soaked in three "milks" of heavy cream, condensed milk, and evaporated milk. *Arroz con leche* is a rice pudding flavored with sugar and spices.

29

Glossary

embargo   A ban on trading with another country.

military   A group created by the government that protects a country and fights in wars.

private ownership   When land or a business is owned by one or more citizens instead of the government.

ration   A fixed amount of food people are allowed during a time of shortage.

saint   A person who is remembered for being good or holy.

slave   A person who is owned or controlled by another person.

socialist   Relating to a system where the government controls the economy and provides services to the people.

Find Out More

Books

Engle, Margarita. *Drum Dream Girl: How One Girl's Courage Changed Music*. New York, NY: HMH Books for Young Readers, 2015.

Wells, Rosemary. *My Havana: Memories of a Cuban Boyhood*. Somerville, MA: Candlewick, 2010.

Website

National Geographic Kids: Cuba Country Profile

kids.nationalgeographic.com/explore/countries/

cuba/#/cuba-matanzas.jpg

Video

Cuba with Kids: Havana Highlights

www.youtube.com/watch?v=ZJq4eJH5zL0

This video provides a closer look at Havana.

Index

About the Author

Laura L. Sullivan is the author of more than forty fiction and nonfiction books for children, including the fantasies *Under the Green Hill* and *Guardian of the Green Hill*. She lives in Florida where she likes to bike, hike, kayak, hunt fossils, and practice Brazilian jiujitsu.